The Weighted Heart

Lacie Shea

To the hearts I've wanted, known and lost.

THE FANTASY

He smelled of daydreams and sin
and everything she wanted to run to.

If only I could touch you...
I could light a thousand flames with that one spark.

Let's run somewhere between here and there
and imagine distance won't chase us.

I know it wasn't real, but this pain...
It touches *everything*.

And maybe one morning we'll meet, under a California sun,
outside a used bookstore, with smiles on our faces
and coffees in our hands.

Let's run and fuel our sins with
secrets, sex and poetry.

At night, I imagine it's your lips that brush my skin; not the sheets. That your weight comforts my body; not the blankets. That you're disappearing into me; not into my fantasies.

I want to lose you deep in my memory,
so that I may look for you always.

You've never crossed my lips,
but my heart can speak of nothing else.

Restless with thoughts of you...
If only we could toss and turn together.

Run away with me. I'll feed you love and tell you stories
of all the things I've imagined we could be.

We exist in hotel sheets, late nights and pancakes at noon.

Stay with me in this fantasy; it's so much safer here.

My fingers itch to touch you, but my thoughts feel you like silk.

I think about telling you,
but then I'd have to stop talking to you.

If only your words could touch my body,
like they do my heart.

We were butterflies. We were daydreams. We were fantasies. We were everything. We were impossible.

If we could...would you?

Fingers laced. Legs entwined. Lips locked.
Tongues twisted. Toes curled.
Oh... To be tangled in you.

My body begs for sleep, while my heart
stays up to entertain thoughts of you.

I want to read your body like braille.
Every touch revealing just a little more.

I'm happy to dance around the edges with you.

Lacie Shea

There's you. There's me. There's reality.
Let's have fun with the fantasy.

Practice makes perfect and still,
I slip when walking the line between fantasy and reality.

I know you're not mine, but my fantasies feel differently.

From time to time, I allow myself to disappear into the *what if.*

The anticipation of you; I think I could hold my breath forever.

Fate gives her both permission and an excuse.

Possibility is my favorite thing to flirt with.

When I'm good, I'm really good.
But when I'm bad...*I'm better.*

The guilt might kill me, but God...
It'd be an amazing way to go.

THE LOVE

My eyes traced the ink that wrapped his arm.
I'd never known a man to wear his heart on a sleeve so beautifully.

The return of rain, like a lover she thought gone.
The smell, the gratitude, the release.
How she longed to stay in bed and soak in all she'd missed.

Lacie Shea

You exist in my poems. In the words, in the spaces between; in all that is said and all that isn't

You hear everything I'm too afraid to say.

I melted into your hands and asked you to make me beautiful.

Because of you, I ask the questions I forgot I wanted answers to.

There's a beauty in coincidences, how they fall in line
and allow the impossible to take shape.

I have never felt more beautiful than in
the warm shirt I found, lost between the sheets you left.

You remind me of tobacco and vanilla, August clouds and love songs, gypsy tattoos and heartache.

I crave you like sunshine. The heat of your skin.
The light in your eyes. And kisses that turn me red.

Come back to bed with me.
I didn't sleep last night, why sleep now?

How lucky I am to hold the hand that holds me.

I argue with the morning, because it steals you from me.

"I don't love you." She said,
with fingers crossed behind her back.

Sometimes it feels as though my heart knows nothing but you.

You've made blush my favorite color.

I held my breath to dive in deeper with you.

I hadn't realized all the pieces I'd dropped,
until you put them back.

He saw beauty in all she kept hidden.

While lost in you, I found myself.

Lacie Shea

I'm continually starved, no matter how much of you I devour.

I didn't fall for you. I *jumped*.

You fell for the me I'd forgotten.

We learned more about each other
in the glow of a muted movie, then in the flicker of candlelight.

Maybe it was just a string of coincidences, but the way it tied them together; they seemed made for each other.

THE LOSS

Lacie Shea

My mind jumps from memory to memory of you,
afraid to lose you in the cracks between.

I watch you from behind this glass,
wondering if you see me and the hearts I draw
in the fog of my breath.

She'd given so much of her love away that she felt like a thief when she tried to keep some for herself.

I talk to you in poems, dreaming of the day, I'll talk to you again.

At night when my thoughts scream your name,
I wonder if they're loud enough to wake you.

And there we sat, hands wrapped around empty glasses,
drained of all we'd been carrying, hoping for another round.

I slid your shirt over me, the way I used to slide over you. I held
my arms around me, the way I used to hold you. I breathed in
my memories, the way I used to breathe in you.
I never want to let go, unlike the way, I let go of you.

The look in your eyes as you walked away;
it was as if your heart was being held hostage.

Lacie Shea

Like dusty, August sidewalks; she prayed for rain,
a fresh start and something different.

The weight of your memory lies heavy across my chest.
Even gone, you steal my breath.

I'm sure it's my heart, but oh,
this ache...
I feel it everywhere.

My mind flips through memories of you like my favorite book. I catch glimpses of parts I loved. I pause to revisit things I didn't understand. And I fold back corners on moments I hope to never forget.

I hate that my mind said good-bye, before my heart had the chance.

I wanted the impossible. I wanted you.

I miss you. It's that simple and that complex.

I give you all my thoughts, knowing you won't return the favor.

My mind and my heart are at it again. And honestly,
I don't feel like talking to either of them.

Tell me unfiltered truths and I'll believe what I want.

Day crept in and stole you from me.

Her sad blue eyes saw his tears; more pain,
more heartbreak, more salt in her wounds.

Lacie Shea

She noticed the dust collecting on their picture;
how long had she too been unseen, untouched, unloved.

She righted her devil horns and smiled.
How good it felt to no longer give a fuck.

I want it back. Every piece I gave you.
I will put myself back together.
I will make myself whole.

I heard you, but your actions had a lot more to say.

I've stopped counting every time you say, "I love you"
and have started counting every time you miss your chance.

Please, even a whispered, "I love you."
The world doesn't need to know,
just me.

Lacie Shea

And finally, my heart's run out of excuses for why you're not here.

And she promised this was the last time, just one more time.

Lacie Shea

It's not my back I'm turning, it's the page.
I don't rip pages from stories I love.

Let's ignore the sunset and imagine
we still have hours left in the warmth of the sun.

My heart has begun to see that my brain
has some very valuable points.

Look at you with all your compartments. How nice it must be to have a place to keep everything.

If only I could drink time from a glass. It seems alcohol isn't strong enough to forget you.

She longed for kept promises, simple decisions
and unquestionable love.

Lacie Shea

I wonder why you don't ask, and then I think,
it's probably the same reason I don't tell.

She'd already started packing;
her stories, her dreams, her confessions, her heart.
It was clear, he wasn't her home.

Love me like you promised. Love me like you know me.
Love me like you want me. Love me like I love you.

My memories of you are wearing thin,
I can't wait to trade them in.

I touch your calloused hands and consider all they've carried;
maybe it's the weight of my heart that's caused the most damage.

Oh the exhaustion of night.
If only my demons turned off as easily as the light.

Time. Time is the answer.
I need it. I can give it.
What's left, but to take it.

I wanted to kiss the wind; capture it between my fingers
and hold it against me. The smell, the warmth,
all the memories of you blowing right through.

It kills me to know you're not my forever,
knowing how much I love you now.

When I close my eyes,
I go back to you and all the promises made.

I don't fit into your world, but I'd like to think
there's a place for me in your heart.

I waited to open my eyes. I knew you were gone,
but I wasn't ready to see the light.

To you I was simply a stand-in, a substitute, a placeholder.
Something to replace; never someone to keep.

I miss the moments, from before, I missed you.

It's different now, I'm no longer a stranger.
I'm no longer the girl you thought you wanted.

You stepped back a little and I rushed to love you a little more.

How silly for you to think I'd write for you,
when you were never right for me.

I am worth so much more than you're willing to pay.

Lacie Shea

We are nothing more than countless conversations
and missed opportunities.

"It's over." She said, pulling him to bed.

And I wondered if I was your escape.
Something to run through, instead of someone to run to.

At first taste your lies were deliciously sweet; but I over ate and now, even the thought of them makes me sick.

I needed you and you needed that.

You didn't say goodnight and I wondered
if there'd be a good morning.

You are forever wrapped in fantasy. A deliciously sexy, passionate, what if world that I can't help but crave from time to time. And then I convince myself it's ok to blur the lines, if only to escape for a heartbeat.

Tell me there's a little heartbreak when you think of me. If I can't be with you, don't let me be alone in that.

Please turn out the light. The only way for me to find you
is in the dark.

I knew it wasn't real, but my heart couldn't resist playing pretend.

There's something different in the air,
maybe that's why the butterflies left.

You're locked in my heart; my tears your only escape.

I want to go back to the fantasy.
I want to go back to when you loved me.

I can hear you so clearly in your silence.

I wish the world could stop, so we could keep going.

I told you too much, too fast.
I wanted you to have all of me, even if
I could only collect fragments of you.

The complexity of love is simple. It's simply complex.

I know I'll see you again.
Even the moon and the sun cross paths occasionally.

Tell me a story, but make it a happy ending this time;
something different from us.

I see you in dreams, in second guesses,
in missed opportunities, but never in person.

I clawed at you from inside my cage desperate for a piece.
I knew I could never have the whole, but I still wanted a taste.

I allowed myself the pleasure of tasting possibility,
while ignoring the bitter truth.

How maddening that my head continues to fill with you,
while my arms have nothing to hold.

I sleep better with you in my bed,
then I do with you running through my head.

A thousand times I've forgiven you,
without once hearing an apology.

I fed your ego, hoping to get full.

I told you everything I wanted to hear.
I only wish I'd been the one listening.

When the memory of you was more familiar than the person standing in front of me, that's when I knew.

I mistook city lights for the stars.

Want and need, never have.

Do you remember what I can't forget?

I want to go back to the girl he wanted.
The girl he chased. The girl he couldn't have.
I want the me, before the him.

Lacie Shea

It's hard to see the bigger picture,
when I'm continually drawn to you.

I believed in magic, until your disappearing act.

I'm still here...but you knew that already

I'm done crediting you for my strength.
You may have been the spark, but I fanned the flame.

Lacie Shea

When the heart wins, it's the brain that says I told you so.

You broke my heart and still I feed you the pieces.

I always knew we'd fade.
I'm just grateful we had the chance to glow.

I didn't realize I was being used, until I was used up.

She's stuck counting down to something that once was.

Why would I meet you in this lifetime,
when we'd only ever work in another?

Forever was never us. We were more for now.

How strange to know there was a we without an us.

She let go, but dug her nails into the memories.

I didn't think I could want anything as bad as a kiss
and then...*you left*.

It's not the miles between us, it's the distance.

There was the before and the after, but
oh...the during

Lacie Shea

Some nights the moon is too bright,
the distant barking too loud, the bedroom air too hot.
Most nights, it's the absence of you.

What changed that made everything different?

Just tell me once more that I was the one.
One more text. One more call. One more moment

I knew you weren't coming home,
but I couldn't turn out the light.

You're always there, you're just never here.

We were so deep, now we barely scratch the surface.

And maybe one day, we'll sit across from one another,
share a knowing smile and shake our heads
at the pure craziness of it all.

Can we start over? I hate to lose.

If this is it, please stay,
because I can't let go.

And maybe that's what allowed us to fall,
we weren't caught in reality.

She kept their secret, but wanted to keep him.

I'm on a first name basis with my memories of you.

She kept running long after he'd crossed the finish line.

Of all the lies, the ones I've told myself are the hardest to forgive.

What I thought it was, was different from what it ever was.

When I no longer believed in your ghost.
That's when you came back to haunt me.

How am I to navigate this earth without you,
when you are the only one who speaks my language.

I can feel time lifting each finger.
How good it will feel to finally let go.

"Why?" He asked.
"Because even a broken heart still beats." She said.

I see now that I loved you more,
but it doesn't make me love you any less.

How did we have such different definitions of always.

How forgetful we both are.
You forgot me and I forgot to let go.

How can I not pull back, when my heart is being pulled in two?

I saw it coming, just as clouds hint at storms.

You couldn't catch me, but you softened the fall.

The dark turns up the volume on my memories of you.

The heart is the only thing that weighs more,
when it holds less.

You're gone and my tears fall as easily as I fell in love.

My heart's won races I should have never entered.

I've imagined a million ways to say I love you,
if I'm ever given that one chance.

The heat of your skin, left burn marks on my heart.

You wanted it to be easy. That's how I knew it wasn't love.

Save the apology. We both know we'll be back.

I know you still care. I left you with a piece of my heart
and there's no way it'd forget me.

And so, it seems... "You break it. You buy it"
doesn't apply to the heart.

Look at the mess I made. I poured out all of my feelings
with no way to clean them up.

The less I speak, the louder my heart screams.

I told you the truth, then wondered if I was lying to myself.

Your eyes held me tighter than hands ever could.

I still wear the shirt you gave me. It's lost your scent,
but I like that it was yours; like I used to be.

I talk to you in poems, dreaming of the day,
I'll talk to you again.

I saw your new tattoo.
It hurts to know that there is a piece of you
my fingers haven't traced.

You've become a fictional character;
someone from a movie I fell in love with;
a make-believe person I write love letters to.

You told me I was easy to love.
But it seems, I'm even easier to forget.

Let's pretend reality isn't against us
and that fate is on our side.

You get these poems.
And I get to wonder if you read them.

Made in the USA
Lexington, KY
06 December 2019

58252294R00116